DRUGS
METHAMPHETAMINE AND AMPHETAMINES

A MyReportLinks.com Book

David Aretha OCT 2 4 2006

MyReportLinks.com Books

an imprint of

Enslow Publishers, Inc. E

Box 398, 40 Industrial Road
Berkeley Heights, NJ 07922
USA

MyReportLinks.com Books, an imprint of Enslow Publishers, Inc. MyReportLinks®
is a registered trademark of Enslow Publishers, Inc.

Library of Congress Cataloging-in-Publication Data

Aretha, David.
  Methamphetamine and amphetamines / David Aretha.
    p. cm. — (Drugs)
  Includes bibliographical references and index.
  ISBN 0-7660-5279-6
  1. Amphetamines—Juvenile literature. 2. Methamphetamine—Juvenile literature. 3. Amphetamine abuse—
Juvenile literature. 4. Methamphetamine abuse—Juvenile literature. I. Title. II. Drugs (Berkeley Heights, N.J.)
  RA1242.A5A74 2005
  362.29'9—dc22
                                        2004009000

Printed in the United States of America

10 9 8 7 6 5 4 3 2

To Our Readers:
Through the purchase of this book, you and your library gain access to the Report Links that specifically back
up this book.
The Publisher will provide access to the Report Links that back up this book and will keep these Report Links
up to date on **www.myreportlinks.com** for five years from the book's first publication date.
We have done our best to make sure all Internet addresses in this book were active and appropriate when we went
to press. However, the author and the Publisher have no control over, and assume no liability for, the material
available on those Internet sites or on other Web sites they may link to.
The usage of the MyReportLinks.com Books Web site is subject to the terms and conditions stated on the Usage
Policy Statement on **www.myreportlinks.com**.
A password may be required to access the Report Links that back up this book. The password is found on the
bottom of page 4 of this book.
Any comments or suggestions can be sent by e-mail to comments@myreportlinks.com or to the address on the
back cover.

Photo Credits: AP/Wide World Photos, pp. 1, 12, 16, 36; © 1999–2004 by *KCI The Anti-Meth Site,* p. 31;
© 2004 Partnership for a Drug-Free America, pp. 28, 33; © 2004 The Mentor Foundation International, p. 41;
MyReportLinks.com Books, p. 4; National Archives, p. 39; National Institute on Drug Abuse, p. 25;
Photos.com, pp. 3 (cold pills), 43; U.S. Department of Health and Human Services/The National Institute
on Drug Abuse, p. 22; U.S. Drug Enforcement Administration, pp. 3 (bag and white pills), 9, 10, 13, 15, 19,
20, 27, 37.

Cover Photo: AP/Wide World Photos (main image); U.S. Drug Enforcement Administration (bag).

Cover Description: Law enforcement officers clean up a suspected meth lab.

Disclaimer: While the stories of abuse in this book are real, many of the names have been changed.

MyReportLinks.com Books
Great Books, Great Links, Great for Research!

The Internet sites listed on the next four pages can save you hours of research time. These Internet sites—we call them "Report Links"—are constantly changing, but we keep them up to date on our Web site.

Give it a try! Type http://www.myreportlinks.com into your browser, click on the series title, then the book title, and scroll down to the Report Links listed for this book.

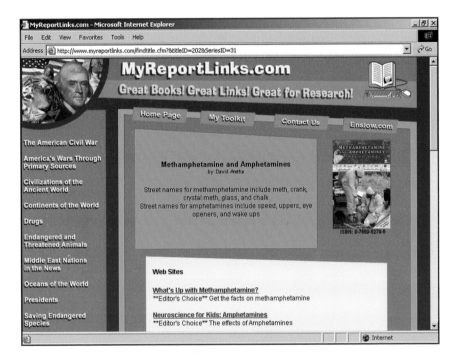

The Report Links will bring you to great source documents, photographs, and illustrations. MyReportLinks.com Books save you time, feature Report Links that are kept up to date, and make report writing easier than ever!

Please see "To Our Readers" on the copyright page for important information about this book, the MyReportLinks.com Web site, and the Report Links that back up this book.

Please enter **DRM2903** if asked for a password.

The Internet sites described below can be accessed at
http://www.myreportlinks.com

*EDITOR'S CHOICE

▶**What's Up with Methamphetamine**
At this Web site you will see what methamphetamine looks like and
learn where it comes from. You will find information on how it is used,
its nicknames, and the mental and physical effects it has on people.

*EDITOR'S CHOICE

▶**Neuroscience for Kids: Amphetamines**
This short article notes the history of amphetamines. Topics covered
include the reasons why people use these drugs and what their effects
are on the body. Read how amphetamines stimulate the central nervous
system. An interactive quiz is also included.

*EDITOR'S CHOICE

▶**Tips for Teens: The Truth About Methamphetamine**
This Web site gives a clear picture of the effects, signs, and risks involved
in using methamphetamine. There is a brief question-and-answer section
written specifically for young people.

*EDITOR'S CHOICE

▶**Methamphetamine**
Methamphetamine quickly and powerfully stimulates the brain. Learn
more about the effects and uses of this drug. Be sure to click on the link
to the article about meth labs.

*EDITOR'S CHOICE

▶**What are Amphetamines and Stimulants?**
Learn what amphetamines and stimulants are, as well as their history,
effects, and street names. Images and a quiz are also included. Follow
the links on the left side of the screen to see the entire article.

*EDITOR'S CHOICE

▶**What is Methamphetamine?**
At this Web site you will learn what methamphetamine is and what
it does to the brain. Its effects are both immediate and long-lasting.
Methamphetamine hurts people and the communities they live in. Test
your knowledge by taking the quiz.

Report Links

The Internet sites described below can be accessed at http://www.myreportlinks.com

▶**About Substance-Related Disorders**

Some teenagers will stop taking drugs after a few tries while others will continue a life of addiction. What are the symptoms of addiction? Why does it happen? How is it treated? Get the answers to these questions at this Web site.

▶**Amphetamine**

Amphetamines were widely used to keep soldiers alert in World War II, long before we knew about their addictive and destructive nature. Long-distance truckers began taking the drug to help them stay awake. Learn more about the uses and effects of amphetamines.

▶**Better Health Channel: Amphetamines**

Drugs like amphetamines speed up activity in the brain and other parts of the central nervous system. In small doses, amphetamines can make us feel full of energy, refreshed, and alert, but after a while these effects will be replaced with irritability, exhaustion, nervousness, and depression.

▶**The Brain's Response to Methamphetamine**

On this Web site, you can find information on the effects methamphetamine has on the brain.

▶**Comparison of Substance Use in Australia and the United States**

Who uses more drugs: American teenagers or Australian teenagers? What types of drugs do they prefer? How old are the users? Find out the answers to these questions, and see how drugs are a worldwide problem.

▶**Drugs: What You Should Know**

Developed for young children, this fact sheet explains what amphetamines and methamphetamines are and what they are sometimes called. It also provides information on how these drugs are used, their addictive nature, and how they affect the body.

▶**Drugs of Abuse: Methamphetamine**

Methamphetamine is a stimulant that affects the central nervous system. Find out more about this drug from this Web site.

▶**FactLine on Amphetamines**

Read about amphetamines and how methamphetamine causes serious health threats. You will learn about "look-alike" drugs and the legal issues surrounding them.

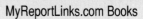
Report Links

The Internet sites described below can be accessed at http://www.myreportlinks.com

▶**Life or Meth?**

This Web site provides information on methampetamine, its effects, and resources for getting help.

▶**Making Prevention Effective for Adolescent Boys and Girls**

Different strategies of the prevention and treatment of drug abuse are used depending on whether they are aimed at boys or girls. Learn more at this Web site.

▶**Mentor Foundation**

The Mentor Foundation seeks to promote the well-being and health of young people around the world. It offers information, support, and effective strategies that will prevent children and teens from ever using drugs.

▶**Methamphetamine: What is it and Why is it Dangerous?**

This four-part article describes the dangers of using methamphetamine, including the way the drug damages brain tissue and changes how the brain works.

▶**Methamphetamine Addiction**

Tweaking occurs when a methamphetamine abuser is coming down from a binge and is feeling uncomfortable, depressed, and empty. Learn more about the different dangers involved for both the tweaker and others so that you can stay safe.

▶**Methamphetamine and Amphetamines**

This Web site offers a variety of information on methamphetamine and amphetamines. Learn who uses these drugs and how much they pay for them. Maps of methamphetamine lab seizure locations are also included.

▶**Methamphetamine: Frequently Asked Questions**

Find out how methamphetamine is made and where a high concentration of laboratories are in the United States. Is there a lab in your neighborhood? Find out the warning signs and a lot more at this Web site.

▶**Methamphetamine Treatment Project**

The Methamphetamine Treatment Project offers many articles and presentation about methamphetamine and treatment for addiction. Pending legislation, links to relevant Web sites, and more is offered here.

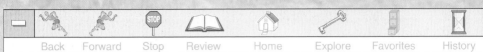
▶**Middlebury College: Amphetamines**

Symptoms of amphetamine use include nausea, hypertension, dizziness, paranoid schizophrenia, hallucinations, weight loss, and insomnia. Learn more signs of use and abuse of amphetamines at this Web site.

▶**NAADAC, The Association for Addiction Professionals**

NAADAC focuses on drug, tobacco, alcohol, and gaming addictions in an effort to create healthier families and communities through prevention, intervention, and quality treatment. The organization supports research, policies, and funding for the prevention, understanding, and treatment of addictions.

▶**Narcotics Anonymous**

Narcotics Anonymous, an international nonprofit organization dedicated to treating drug addiction, can be found in over one hundred countries. Follow the links to find worldwide contact and meeting information. Bulletins, reports, and periodicals are also available to the reader.

▶**NIDA InfoFacts: Methamphetamine**

Methamphetamine is made illegally in hidden laboratories, and has street names such as crank, meth, and ice. You will learn about the health hazards of using the drug and the extent of its use among the adolescent population.

▶**ONDCP Fact Sheet: Methamphetamine**

Information is provided on the background, effects, and use of methamphetamine. Availability of the drug, production, trafficking, legal consequences, as well as information on addiction treatment are included. Street terms are noted.

▶**Partnership for a Drug-Free America**

The Partnership for a Drug-Free America focuses its efforts on reducing substance abuse in America. You will find a recent study on teen drug use, an e-newsletter you can sign up for, and stories of real people.

▶**Research Report Series: Methamphetamine Abuse and Addiction**

The scope of methamphetamine abuse in the United States and how the drug is used are both covered in this report. You can also read about the short-term and long-term effects of methamphetamine abuse, medical complications, and effective treatments.

▶**What You Need to Know About Drugs: Methamphetamines**

This fact sheet explains what methamphetamine is and how it is used. It also provides information on what methamphetamine does to you as well as slang names for the drug.

METHAMPHETAMINE AND AMPHETAMINES

✗ Worldwide, more than 30 million people abuse amphetamine-type stimulants.

✗ The production and distribution of amphetamine-type stimulants is a $65 billion-a-year business.

✗ According to a 2002 survey, 5.3 percent of the United States population—more than 12 million people—reported having tried methamphetamine at least once in their lifetime.

✗ Based on a 2003 study, 6.2 percent of high school seniors and 3.9 percent of eighth graders had tried methamphetamine during their lifetime.

✗ According to one survey, 48.7 percent of American high school seniors did not think it would be a great risk to try crystal meth once or twice.

✗ More than 90 percent of people who regularly take methamphetamine become addicted to it.

✗ Emergency department mentions of methamphetamine rose from 10,447 in 1999 to 17,696 in 2002.

✗ The United States Drug Enforcement Administration reported more than nine thousand raids of methamphetamine labs from October 2001 to October 2002.

✗ The sale and use of methamphetamine accounts for up to 90 percent of all drug cases in many Midwest communities.

✗ A person caught with amphetamine or methamphetamine, even on a first offense, could face up to a year in prison.

✗ Federal law mandates a five-year prison sentence for anyone who sells five to forty-nine grams of methamphetamine.

Chapter 1

SPEED, METH, AND DEATH

After running away from home at age sixteen, Holly* wound up at a house full of addicts. There, a tall man offered her a hit of her favorite drug: methamphetamine. For the next several weeks, Holly lived in the man's meth house. The place smelled of urine, smoke, and chemicals. Cats urinated on mounds of dirty clothes. Rats skittered along the floor. Men abused the home's women, who stayed because they were addicted to meth. "People were always screaming," Holly remembered. "Either they were getting the crap beat out of them or being raped."[1]

Holly wore the same pair of clothes for weeks. She sold meth to support her habit. She caught scabies, and her weight dropped

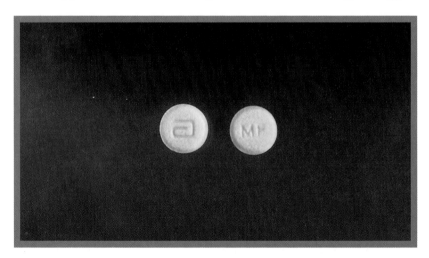

▲ *Methamphetamine (shown here) is a highly addictive drug. The government classifies it as a Schedule II drug. This means that while the drug is used by doctors to treat certain conditions, methamphetamine is likely to be abused by users who develop a severe psychological or physical dependence on it.*

*While the stories of abuse in this book are real, many of the names have been changed.

to seventy-five pounds. (Having scabies is like having mites over your entire body. They eventually live under a person's skin and cause hideous sores.) "I lived on sugar and cocoa packets," she said. "Every penny went for drugs or cigarettes."[2]

Holly narrowly escaped death after two men fouled up a meth recipe. The mixture of chemicals nearly caused an explosion. On another occasion, Holly saw a teenager suffer a drug-induced seizure with the needle still in his arm. She was not sure if he died, but she had heard rumors of backyard burials.

Finally, police picked up Holly as she wandered around outside. She had been awake—and high—for seventeen straight days. She eventually survived a grueling rehabilitation program. But, she added, "I will battle this craving until the day I die."[3]

A National Epidemic

All across America, amphetamine and its more potent derivative, methamphetamine, are destroying lives. Each drug is a powerful stimulant. Amphetamine (aka "speed" and "uppers") comes in the form of pills, capsules, or powder. Methamphetamine is sold as both a powder ("meth" and "crank") and cooked crystals ("ice" and "glass").

For decades, people have taken amphetamines to achieve euphoria, stay awake, increase energy, or lose weight. In recent years, Americans have abused methamphetamine for similar reasons, but mostly to get high. Both drugs are extremely addictive. Each can lead to organ damage, depression, rage, paranoia, seizures, and death.

Methamphetamine has been called the "crack cocaine of the new millennium." In many states, meth abuse has reached epidemic levels. More than a million Americans each year use methamphetamine—most of them age twenty-three or younger.

"It's incredibly addictive, and the withdrawals are horrendous," said Terri Yaksic, administrative support specialist for the North Central Washington Narcotics Task Force. "For users, all the things

 Two government workers clean up a suspected meth lab in Tennessee. One pound of meth can create five to seven pounds of toxic waste, making these labs hazardous waste sites. Cleaning up a meth lab is costly and is usually done at the property owner's expense.

they hold dear—their children, families, homes—become secondary, and all they want is their next fix. They look double their age in five years."[4]

People can make methamphetamine in their own kitchens using store-bought products. This makes the spread of the drug almost impossible to stop. After raiding eight hundred meth labs in 1995, the U.S. Drug Enforcement Administration (DEA) reported more than nine thousand lab raids over a twelve-month period beginning in 2001. Yet tens of thousands of labs continued to operate.

Tragic Tales

Not everyone obtains their first dose of amphetamines illegally. John was having trouble focusing in school. His doctor mistakenly prescribed him Ritalin, a stimulant similar to amphetamine. Ritalin calms those with attention deficit disorder (ADD), but it stimulates those who do not have ADD—such as John. At first, John thought the pills worked magic. "For the first time in my life I felt I could take on the world and do anything," he wrote. But, he

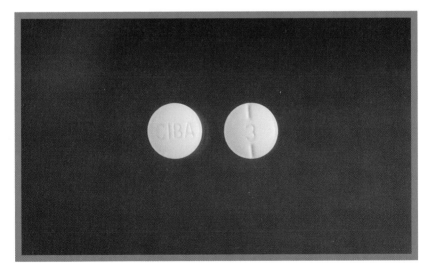

▲ Ritalin is an important drug in treating those with attention deficit disorders. However, this drug has become an object of abuse in recent years. For this reason, the government has classified Ritalin as a Schedule II drug.

added, "as time passed I sunk more into depression even when I was loading up on the Ritalin. I was getting the hallucinations and was wired, paranoid, and jumped up at any noise. Everyone irritated me. I turned into a completely different person."[5]

Due to his addiction to Ritalin, as well as alcohol and cigarettes, John developed acute pancreatitis. "My eyes and skin were yellow because my liver was failing," he wrote. His kidneys were severely damaged, too. "I also got the news," he added, "that I have high blood pressure and my heart was enlarged, which I knew was because of the Ritalin abuse." John realized that he probably would die young—because of his addiction to drugs. "My only wish [is that] I could go back to the start and make it right," he said.[6]

Methamphetamine is ruining the lives of users and their loved ones. Said Jackie of her meth-addicted nephew, "He'll just stare out the door for over an hour. . . . He's twitching all the time, sloppy in his appearance and manner, talks about sores up his nose, wears sunglasses all the time, has a high-and-mighty attitude. I'm just so angry."[7]

Jasmine and Rocky of Albuquerque, New Mexico, can relate to Jackie's feelings. In the 1990s, the couple burst with pride over their three teenage children. Each lived a clean life and excelled in high school sports. Yet after graduation, each became addicted to methamphetamine. Two of them dropped out of college. They

PERCENTAGE REPORTING METHAMPHETAMINE USE, BY AGE GROUP, 2002			
AGE GROUP	LIFETIME	ANNUAL	PAST 30 DAYS
12–17	1.5%	0.9%	0.3%
18–25	5.7%	1.7%	0.5%
26–34	6.7%	1.0%	0.5%
35 and up	5.5%	0.3%	0.1%
12 and up total	5.3%	0.7%	0.3%

*Source: Substance Abuse and Mental Health Services Administration

▲ *The methamphetamine ice crystals in this bag appear to be as harmless as sugar. Yet some users would even steal from their families to get what is in this bag.*

became withdrawn and often volatile around their mom and dad. Then they ignored them altogether. "The hardest was Mother's Day two years ago when none of my children were around," Jasmine recalled in 2004. "We were so close. . . ."[8]

Jasmine drove through the worst neighborhoods of Albuquerque looking for her kids. "I mostly just sat in my car and cried all night," she said.[9] She eventually found her oldest daughter in a hospital, the victim of a meth overdose. Her son wound up in jail, his home for more than a hundred days. Her youngest daughter, age twenty and the mother of a toddler, was still on the streets somewhere.

Unless something is done, "you will see a generation of brain-damaged people," said Paul Brethen, director of a drug research and treatment office. "We are losing sanity and destroying potential."[10]

HISTORY OF SPEED AND METH

Country music legend Johnny Cash was a man's man. "We're all sissies in comparison," said U2's Bono.[1] Yet in the 1960s, Cash gave in to a weakness for amphetamines. "I honestly thought it was a blessing," he said, "a gift from God, these pills were." As it turned out, he said, they were "the devil in disguise."[2]

Cash's drug use destroyed his marriage. He tore up motel rooms, crashed his car, and wound up in jail several times. One night, a law officer in Georgia arrested Cash and confronted him. "My wife is a big fan of yours," the man told Cash. "When I went

▲ *Johnny Cash (left) talks with an inmate at Folsom Prison in 1968 after recording his hit album* Johnny Cash at Folsom Prison. *Three years earlier, Cash had been arrested for smuggling amphetamines into the country from Mexico in his guitar case.*

home last night and told her I had Johnny Cash in my jail, she cried all night."[3]

Cash eventually remarried, and turned his career around. His new wife, June Carter, helped him kick his addictions. It was, however, a long struggle.

For decades, amphetamines have brought the strongest and healthiest people to the lowest of depths. The story of speed and meth is a long, sad, tragic tale.

History of Amphetamine

People have taken stimulants for centuries. In South America, ancient natives chewed coca leaves for bursts of energy. Caffeine is another type of stimulant. Every day, hundreds of millions of people sip coffee for an early-morning eye-opener. Amphetamine, though, is a more potent and more dangerous stimulant than caffeine.

Amphetamine is short for alpha-methyl-phenyl-ethyl-amine. It is available in pills, capsules, and tablets. Amphetamine sulfate, a white crystalline substance, can be snorted. The drug also can be dissolved and injected into the bloodstream, which produces a stronger high and more physical damage.

Created in Germany in 1887, amphetamine was first tested on humans in the 1920s. The amphetamine Benzedrine hit the market in the 1930s to treat a variety of illnesses: narcolepsy, hyperactivity, asthma, depression, and seasickness. Some users enjoyed the pleasurable side effects of this new "wonder drug." During World War II, militaries supplied some types of amphetamine to soldiers. The drug kept them awake and increased their energy and morale. British soldiers were supplied more than 70 million amphetamine pills. Nazi leader Adolf Hitler took several injections of amphetamine each day.

When American servicemen returned after the war, many were addicted to a variety of amphetamines. Nevertheless, the drug became popular in the United States. Doctors, who thought the pills were relatively harmless, prescribed them freely. Many people who

REPORTED METHAMPHETAMINE USE BY ARRESTEES, 2003

PAST METHAMPHETAMINE USE BY ARRESTEES	MALE	FEMALE
Used in past seven days	4.0%	9.0%
Used in past thirty days	4.7%	11.3%
Used in past year	7.7%	15.3%
Average number of days used in past thirty days	7.1 days	8.4 days

*Source: National Institute of Justice

worked or studied at night, such as truck drivers and college students, popped "pep pills" to stay awake. Housewives took them to battle fatigue, depression, and weight gain. In the 1950s and 1960s, amphetamines became a widely used recreational drug among "hip" groups such as the beatniks and mods. In 1964, the drug became illegal in the United States without a prescription, but abuse continued. Teenagers took them to get high, often stealing the pills from their parents' medicine chests.

By the early 1970s, billions of amphetamine pills were produced legally each year. However, doctors were becoming more conscious of the bad side effects of the drug, such as addiction, anxiety, violent behavior, and organ damage. To limit the drug, the United States government imposed quotas on production of amphetamines. Still, the drug remained popular.

As people's lives became busier, many Americans turned to amphetamines as a shortcut to stay awake in hopes of getting more things done. In 1982, for example, 18 percent of those age thirteen to twenty-five took amphetamines. Young women popped diet pills to stay thin, while athletes took amphetamines to increase their energy. In the late 1980s and 1990s, speed became a popular drug at raves, concerts, and parties. A number of these users took speed with alcohol and other drugs—then wound up in the emergency room or county morgue. By the beginning of the

Some amphetamines are  *prescribed by doctors to treat patients with narcolepsy, attention deficit disorder, and/or weight control issues.*

twenty-first century, the problem was as bad as ever: In 2003, about 14.4 percent of twelfth graders nationwide had reported using amphetamines at some point in their lifetime.[4]

History of Methamphetamine

Methamphetamine, a derivative of amphetamine, was developed by Japanese chemists in 1919. It, too, was prescribed by doctors in the 1950s and 1960s, largely to treat depression and obesity. In 1967, American physicians issued 31 million prescriptions for methamphetamine.

In the 1960s, the young counterculture experimented with numerous drugs. One was a new form of meth, an injectable form that was more potent and much more addictive. In 1970, the federal government severely limited the legal production of methamphetamine, but the drug did not disappear. Motorcycle gangs on the West Coast made the drug, used it, and sold it. Meth became known as "crank" because bikers hid the drug in their motorcycles' crank cases.

Methamphetamine users have several options for ingesting the drug. Meth is available in a pill form and as white powder, which is snorted. Methamphetamine hydrochloride comes in the form of clear, chunky crystals and can be inhaled by smoking.

Users commonly refer to this form as "ice" or "glass." Hardcore meth abusers inject a dissolved form of the drug into their body. This form of meth is so potent that some users have dropped dead with the needle still in their arms.

Through the late 1980s, methamphetamine was mostly confined to California and the Southwest. However, word spread that the drug was cheap and pleasurable and had long-lasting effects. Like a disease, meth and ice spread to other regions of the country. Drug dealers in numerous states set up meth labs. Organized crime groups got in on the action, smuggling meth or meth ingredients from Mexico to the United States.

Moreover, non-dealers began making the drug in their homes and garages. They downloaded meth recipes from the Internet and bought ingredients at local stores. In many communities, meth users taught their friends how to make the drug. "For every one that learns to cook, they teach ten," said Marti Reilly, a commander of a Midwest drug task force.[5]

In 1994, an estimated 1.8 million Americans had tried methamphetamine in their lifetime. Three years later, that number skyrocketed to 5.3 million.[6] Thousands of users were young

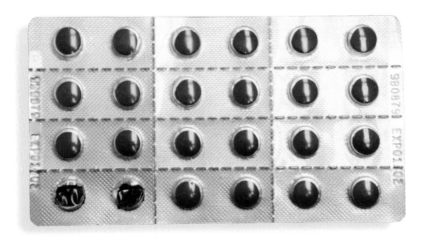

▲ Pseudoephedrine is a chemical found in cold medications that are sold over the counter at many pharmacies. Some people use pseudoephedrine to make methamphetamine.

women and girls who wanted to lose weight. Many did lose weight—up to ten pounds in a week—but were stuck with a life-threatening addiction.

An Epidemic

In some states, meth use reached epidemic proportions. In Washington State, the number of meth lab seizures soared from 38 in 1990 to 1,449 in 2000. In Hawaii, 90 percent of confirmed child abuse cases were related to meth use. Methamphetamine ran rampant in rural Midwestern states, including Iowa, Missouri, and Kansas. In Iowa in 1995, meth arrests accounted for 47 percent of drug-related busts.[7]

While meth destroyed lives and families, states spent millions of dollars to fight meth abuse and treat abusers. It cost thousands of dollars to clean up just one small-scale meth lab. Because of the toxic chemicals, lab raiders had to wear special hazmat (hazardous materials) suits, which look like spacesuits.

Lawmakers tried to crack down on meth use. Congress enacted the Comprehensive Methamphetamine Control Act of 1996. The law controlled the key chemicals needed to produce the drug. It also stiffened sentences for possessing and distributing meth. However, drug dealers and users continued to find ways to abuse methamphetamine. After the ingredient ephedrine was banned, meth makers switched to pseudoephedrine, a chemical found in over-the-counter cold medications.

In the new century, meth use continued to run rampant. Hundreds of people died from its effects each year. Many treatment facilities were so overwhelmed, patients had to join long waiting lists to get in. Captain Peter Groetken, head of the detective force in meth-plagued Sioux City, Iowa, saw no end to the madness. "Each year they make more arrests . . . seize more dope . . . seize more guns, execute more search warrants," he said. "It's not stopping the flow of drugs."[8]

HORRIFIC EFFECTS

Ricky Hogg, a parole officer in Arkansas, saw first hand what methamphetamine could do to people. Hogg accompanied under-cover officers on a raid of a meth house, which was filled with addicts and littered with drug paraphernalia. "In the bathroom was my parolee, trying to shoot up," Hogg said. "He wasn't trying

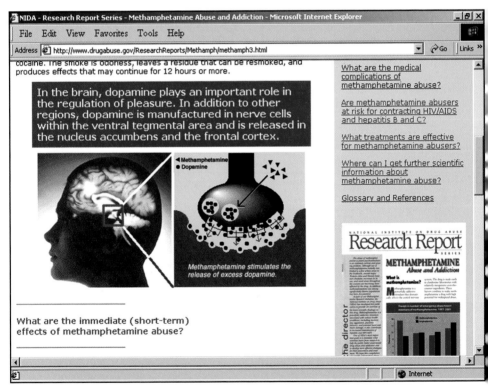

NIDA - Research Report Series - Methamphetamine Abuse and Addiction - Microsoft Internet Explorer

File   Edit   View   Favorites   Tools   Help

Address http://www.drugabuse.gov/ResearchReports/Methamph/methamph3.html   Go   Links »

cocaine. The smoke is odorless, leaves a residue that can be resmoked, and produces effects that may continue for 12 hours or more.

In the brain, dopamine plays an important role in the regulation of pleasure. In addition to other regions, dopamine is manufactured in nerve cells within the ventral tegmental area and is released in the nucleus accumbens and the frontal cortex.

◀ Methamphetamine
● Dopamine

Methamphetamine stimulates the release of excess dopamine.

What are the immediate (short-term) effects of methamphetamine abuse?

What are the medical complications of methamphetamine abuse?

Are methamphetamine abusers at risk for contracting HIV/AIDS and hepatitis B and C?

What treatments are effective for methamphetamine abusers?

Where can I get further scientific information about methamphetamine abuse?

Glossary and References

NATIONAL INSTITUTE ON DRUG ABUSE

Research Report
SERIES

METHAMPHETAMINE
Abuse and Addiction

Internet

▲ Methamphetamine causes the brain to release dopamine, providing the user with a euphoric rush. Snorting the drug will create a three- to five-minute rush while digesting it orally will create a ten- to fifteen-minute high. By smoking methamphetamine, a person's high could last for twelve hours or longer.

METHAMPHETAMINE MENTIONS IN EMERGENCY DEPARTMENTS	
YEAR	**NUMBER**
1994	17,537
1995	15,933
1996	11,002
1997	17,154
1998	11,486
1999	20,477
2000	13,505
2001	14,923
2002	17,696

*Source: Drug Abuse Warning Network

to flush it or get rid of it. All he wanted to do was to just get that last fix before he was arrested."[1]

As powerful stimulants, amphetamine and methamphetamine cause users' heads to feel incredibly euphoric and high. But "what goes up comes down," said a recovering addict. "Meth makes you crazy. You hallucinate. You lie, cheat, steal. Everybody becomes your enemy. Nobody's on your side."[2]

▶ Effects on the Brain

As stimulants, amphetamine and methamphetamine increase the body's heart rate and breathing. However, the drugs' most dramatic effects occur in the brain.

The brain contains a chemical called dopamine, which is critical to a person's well-being. It plays a role in a person's mood, body movements, thinking ability, and experiences of pleasure. When amphetamine enters the brain, it causes a tremendous amount of dopamine (and another chemical called norepinephrine) to be released into the brain. The release of dopamine makes the body feel a great deal of pleasure. The drug also prevents dopamine from leaving the brain, meaning the feelings of pleasure last a long time. With methamphetamine, the effects are similar but stronger. The increase in norepinephrine, many scientists theorize, may cause the alertness and antifatigue effects that speed/meth users feel.

Speed and meth damage the brain's ability to produce the proper amount of dopamine. After a high has worn off, the user's mood will "crash." He becomes tired, irritable, depressed. The brain craves more dopamine, but because of the damage the drug has caused, the brain cannot make enough dopamine on its own. It needs more amphetamine or methamphetamine to trigger the release of the dopamine. The user then satisfies this craving by taking more of the drug. It all becomes part of a vicious cycle, which is called addiction.

Amphetamine and methamphetamine are highly addictive. One-time use of methamphetamine easily could put the user on a path to destruction.

▶ Short-Term Effects

The high from amphetamine or methamphetamine can last minutes or hours, depending on how the drugs are ingested. Taken orally or intranasally (snorted), the drugs produce a euphoria that lasts for hours. By smoking or injecting the drugs, the chemicals reach the brain quicker and with greater force. The user feels a stronger "rush," but the pleasurable effects last for minutes instead of hours.

While high, the user experiences a wide range of sensations. She has greater energy, faster reflexes, and a heightened alertness. Her pupils become dilated, and she may talk rapidly and slur her speech. Her heart rate, breathing rate, and blood pressure all go up. If she were hungry and fatigued before, she is not now. However, her mouth becomes dry, and swallowing and

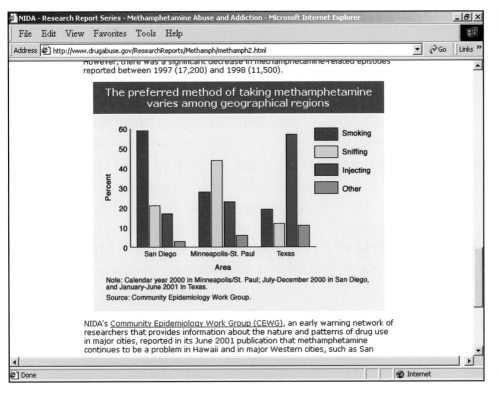

NIDA - Research Report Series - Methamphetamine Abuse and Addiction - Microsoft Internet Explorer

File   Edit   View   Favorites   Tools   Help

Address http://www.drugabuse.gov/ResearchReports/Methamph/methamph2.html

However, there was a significant decrease in methamphetamine-related episodes reported between 1997 (17,200) and 1998 (11,500).

The preferred method of taking methamphetamine varies among geographical regions

Smoking
Sniffing
Injecting
Other

Note: Calendar year 2000 in Minneapolis/St. Paul; July-December 2000 in San Diego, and January-June 2001 in Texas.
Source: Community Epidemiology Work Group.

NIDA's Community Epidemiology Work Group (CEWG), an early warning network of researchers that provides information about the nature and patterns of drug use in major cities, reported in its June 2001 publication that methamphetamine continues to be a problem in Hawaii and in major Western cities, such as San

This chart shows the ways users prefer to take methamphetamine in various parts of the country. Each method has its own set of dangers.

urination become difficult. Also, she can become aggressive and argumentative. High doses of amphetamine can lead to irregular heartbeat, loss of coordination, and physical collapse. Injections cause a dramatic increase in blood pressure, raising the risk of strokes, high fevers, and heart failure.

Again, the effects of meth are much more severe. Users may experience hallucinations and become extremely violent. "They are more paranoid," said Clancy Miller, head of a drug counseling program in San Bernardino, California. "They are fearful and have a sense of impending doom."[3]

Moreover, since most methamphetamine is made by amateurs using toxic chemicals, users never know what they are about to ingest. Many people have become paralyzed, lapsed into a coma, and/or died after consuming poorly made meth.

Binging, Tweaking, and Crashing

Methamphetamine is so powerful that most users cannot limit themselves to a one-time high. Many abusers binge on meth. They maintain their high by smoking or injecting more and more of the drug. During the binge, which could last as long as two weeks, they become mentally and physically hyperactive and require little sleep. Yet each time abusers ingest more of the drug, they experience a weaker rush until there is no high at all. Binging, of course, causes extraordinary damage to their bodies.

Tweaking, which occurs at the end of the binge, is a horrific phase. The user feels extremely agitated, angry, and perhaps paranoid. He takes more meth, but it does not make him feel any better. He might concentrate on a small task for hours. "You open a drawer to clean," said one meth abuser, "and next thing you know you're picking dirt out of the corners."[4]

The tweaker has not eaten or slept properly for days, yet he is not hungry and cannot fall asleep. The feel-good aspects of the drug are long gone. "[At first] you think you're with your best friends in the whole world," said a former homecoming king turned meth abuser. But in the morning, he added, "you hate these people. They disgust you."[5] The tweaker is apt to take a depressant such as alcohol or even heroin to try to feel better, but that just worsens the situation.

Tweakers can be extraordinarily violent. They will physically attack those who irritate them, possibly even their own children. In an extreme case, one meth abuser in New Mexico cut off the head of his fourteen-year-old son. "You're basically not a human being anymore," said Jackie Long of the Bureau of Narcotic Enforcement in Sacramento, California.[6]

Eventually, if they do not die or fall into a coma, meth bingers crash from their high. They become lifeless, sleeping for up to

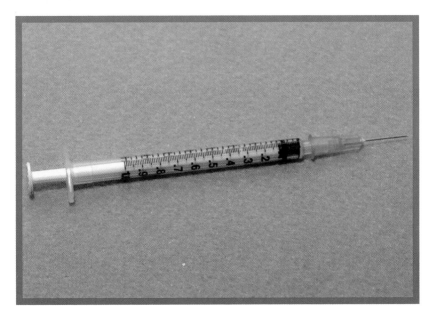

▲ *Many meth users inject the drug in liquid form into their veins using a syringe like the one shown here. Shared syringes place users at risk for contracting HIV and hepatitis B and C.*

three days straight. After the crash, they return to a more stable state, but their systems are not normal. They are addicted to meth, and they have harmed their bodies severely.

▶ Long-Term Effects

From the brain on down, amphetamine and methamphetamine wreak havoc on the body. Prolonged use of the drugs can lead to chronic anxiety, restlessness, and insomnia. Users could develop malnutrition, ulcers, dangerous weight loss, and diseases resulting from vitamin deficiencies. Users may experience confusion, hallucinations, and paranoia or perhaps hypothermia, tremors, and convulsions.

The drugs often harm the vital organs: the liver, kidneys, lungs, and heart. Even young users have suffered fatal heart attacks. Speed and meth can cause irreversible harm to blood vessels in the brain, producing strokes. Users can severely damage their brains and central nervous systems, in some cases permanently. Dr. Greg Hipskind said that because meth decreases the blood flow to the brain, "it dumbs you down."[7]

Many users take other drugs to counteract the effects of speed and meth. This means they can become addicted to multiple drugs. Moreover, combining drugs is highly dangerous and often fatal. While high on meth, users tend to be careless about sex and sharing needles. Thus, they become high-risk candidates for HIV and AIDS as well as unwanted pregnancies. Babies of meth-addicted women suffer through traumatic and painful withdrawals. Many never live a normal life.

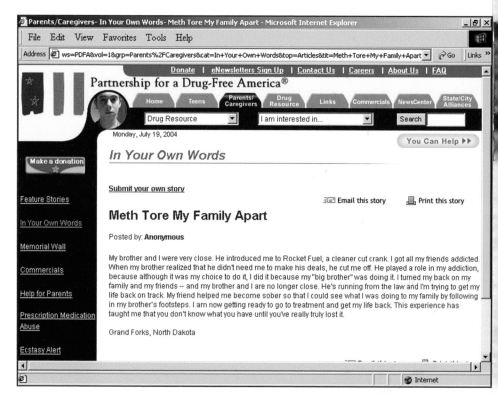

In the past, methamphetamine was most typically used by white, male, blue-collar workers. Studies now show that people of all ages and economic classes are abusing this drug, and tragic stories like the one shown here are becoming all too common.

Desperate for more speed or meth, many users resort to crime to support their habit. They will often steal, prostitute themselves, or physically assault someone for money. Some addicts carry a gun and are not afraid to pull the trigger. Many addicts will sell the drug themselves; as dealers, they risk being locked in prison for years.

Users may fall victim to "Superman Syndrome," thinking they can do anything. This often leads to tragic accidents, including fatal car crashes. Heavy, long-term use may lead to mental illness, including psychosis. Other addicts become terribly violent and aggressive. Some users, feeling so hopeless or ashamed, end up killing themselves.

Effects on Friends and Families

Typically, users harm or destroy the relationships with their loved ones—even their children. According to the *Los Angeles Times,* "Caseworkers have seen baby bottles stored next to poisonous chemicals, infants with meth powder on their clothes and bare feet, children fed the drug to keep them on the same waking cycle as their parents, and addicts as young as 12."[8]

"[Meth] is by far the worst drug I have ever seen," summed up Ben A. Finley, a detective in a narcotics unit in Forsyth County, Georgia. "I tell people this is the closest thing to the devil they will ever see. This drug passes all socioeconomic boundaries (classes and income levels) and it knows no race. It is an equal-opportunity life destroyer."[9]

Chapter 4 ▶

PRODUCING AND SELLING SPEED AND METH

Years ago, methamphetamine was a California problem. "What Colombia is to cocaine, California is to methamphetamine," said Bill Mitchell of the U.S. Drug Enforcement Administration in 1996.[1] Since then, the drug has spread to numerous other states. "Hawaii is being killed," said Edward Kubo, Jr., the U.S. attorney for Hawaii. "We're on our knees right now."[2] Worldwide, more than 30 million people abuse amphetamine-type stimulants. It is a $65 billion-a-year business.

▶ The Market for Amphetamine and Meth

Ask ten drug users why they take uppers or crank, and you might get ten different responses. Amphetamine users are more likely to give "practical" answers. College students: to stay up and study. Factory workers and truck drivers: to stay awake and "alert." Athletes: to improve performance. Fashion models: to cope with pressure and lose weight.

Most who try speed and meth have no clear-cut goal in mind. Many just want to get high and have a good time. Others do it out of the desire to be accepted by others or to escape from their problems. Many concertgoers and partiers take stimulants so they can stay up all night. Some cocaine and heroin users switch to methamphetamine because it is cheaper. Others think meth is less addictive than coke and heroin, but they are wrong. "Nearly 95 percent of all meth users are addicted to the drug after six months of abusing it," said Lieutenant Chan Bailey of the Spokane County Sheriff's Office in Washington.[3]

How They Are Produced

Most amphetamine is made legally, for medical purposes, by pharmaceutical companies. However, some amphetamine sold on the streets is produced illegally in clandestine laboratories. Amphetamine sulphate, a powder, is the most common form of illegally made amphetamine. Dealers mix amphetamine sulphate with other powders, such as caffeine or sugar.

Pharmaceutical companies produce very little methamphetamine. The drug has no legitimate medical uses, except in rare instances of treating obesity. The vast majority of methamphetamine is made in illegal, homemade laboratories. Traditionally,

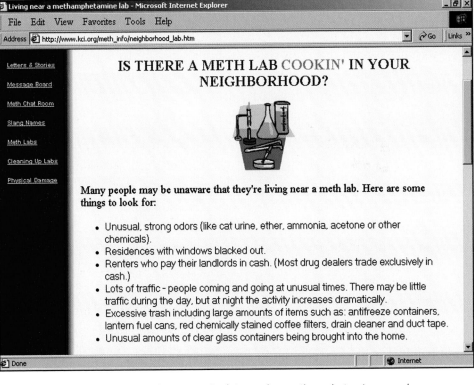

The dangerous procedures required to make methamphetamine can harm those within the clandestine laboratory as well as innocent people in a neighboring house or apartment. If you suspect that there is a meth laboratory in your neighborhood, call the authorities.

most of the methamphetamine sold in the United States was made in California. However, that trend is changing.

Because meth recipes are easy to find, users and dealers are producing the drug throughout the nation. They make it in kitchens, basements, garages, bathtubs, motels, trailers, and abandoned buildings. In 2003, approximately eight thousand illegal meth labs were seized across the country. According to the *Rocky Mountain News,* "Law enforcement officials believe that for every one found, there are 10 others that go undiscovered."[4]

▶ Dirty Cooks

Making methamphetamine is a fairly involved process and very dangerous, but amateurs are able to produce it. To make the drug, meth "cooks" use such over-the-counter ingredients as starter fluid, iodine, and hydrogen peroxide. However, two other ingredients are harder to acquire: anhydrous ammonia and ephedrine (or pseudoephedrine). Cooks may buy both products illegally at super-inflated prices. They also can extract pseudoephedrine from over-the-counter cold medicines. In many meth-plagued communities, stores limit the number of cold medicines they sell to an individual. Yet at large-production meth labs, officials have found as many as three thousand empty bottles of cold medicine.

Meth cooks make the drug for themselves and/or others. On the surface, it is a lucrative business: A one thousand-dollar investment can turn a twenty thousand-dollar profit. Yet the risks are enormous. Cooks work with such dangerous ingredients as rat poison, antifreeze, and drain cleaner. Meth chemists often get sick on toxic chemicals. If something goes afoul, they could blow up their lab and set the building on fire.

Moreover, many toxic chemicals are released during the cooking process. And, said Karen Tandy, head of the U.S. Drug Enforcement Administration, "about 30 percent of the meth labs have children present."[5] Many of these children suffer brain, lung, and kidney damage as well as behavioral problems. Cooks in rural areas tend to dump their toxic chemicals in streams and soil. Such negligence can contaminate communities' water supplies.

Cooks also risk being caught. Methamphetamine gives off a strong, distinct odor, which often raises suspicions of neighbors. It costs about five thousand dollars to bust and clean up a meth lab, but the price tag does not deter law enforcement officials. Communities are furious with meth dealers and are determined to wipe out as many labs as possible.

How They Are Sold

Doctors are cautious about prescribing amphetamine, but it does have legitimate uses. Mainly, it is prescribed to treat obesity and

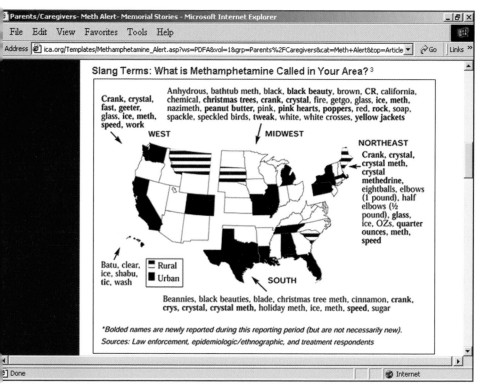

▲ Depending upon where a person lives, he or she may use different slang terms to describe methamphetamine.

ADHD (attention deficit hyperactivity disorder). However, those who want to abuse the drug recreationally buy it illegally from drug dealers or on the Internet.

Young people tend to know who the "drug crowd" is, and those in the drug crowd know dealers. They are often found on college and high school campuses or on street corners in rundown neighborhoods. They also hang around at raves, concerts, and large parties. Some dealers sell amphetamines online. However, many Internet dealers take buyers' money and never send them the drug. Or they will send the buyer an inferior or totally fake form of amphetamine.

Amphetamine sulphate is the most common form of the drug. It goes by such names as "speed," "up," "goey," and "whiz." Compared to other drugs, amphetamine sulphate is inexpensive. It sells for five to ten dollars for a quarter-ounce "wrap."

Methamphetamine pervades California, especially such major cities as Los Angeles, San Diego, and San Francisco. It also infests many less-populated areas across the country. Historically, small-town and small-city residents have not had much access to illegal drugs. Iowa, for example, is a state without many big cities. Yet some of the smaller towns have methamphetamine problems. With methamphetamine, locals can make the drug themselves. "We're in the middle of a meth epidemic," said Ken Carter, director of the Iowa Division of Narcotics Enforcement. "It's from high school all the way up to the age people should know better."[6]

▶ **Dealers Can Be Anywhere**

Many users buy methamphetamine from drug dealers, be it on city street corners or at raves and parties. Others buy meth or ingredients to make the drug on the Internet. In rural areas, users make it themselves or acquire it from a neighbor, friend, or family member. The drug has been called "the poor man's cocaine." Just twenty-five dollars worth of meth can give the user a four-day high.

Despite its low cost, many users spend all of their money on meth. Desperate, they peddle the drug themselves—often to naive teenagers—in order to maintain their habit. The abundance of pushers helps explain why meth abuse has grown at a high rate in recent years.

STREET TERMS

METHAMPHETAMINE	Bathtub crank, Batu, Beannies, Biker's coffee, Black beauty, Blade, Bling bling, Blue devils, Blue meth, Chalk, Chicken feed, Christmas tree meth, Cinnamon, Clear, CR, Crank, Crink, Cris, Cristina, Cristy, Crossles, Crypto, Crystal glass, Crystal Meth, Desocsins, Desogtion, Fast, Geep, Geeter, Getgo, Glass, Go-fast, Granulated orange, Hanyak, Hironpon, Hiropon, Holiday meth, Hot ice, Ice, Kaksonjae, L.A. glass, L.A. ice, Lemon drop, Load of laundry, Meth, Methlies Quick, Mexican crack, Motorcycle crack, Nazimeth, Ozs, Peanut butter, Pink, Pink elephants, Po coke, Poor man's cocaine, Quartz, Redneck cocaine, Rock, Schmiz, Scootie, Shabu, Sketch, Soap dope, Spackle, Sparkle, Speckled birds, Speed, Stove top, Super ice, Tick tick, Trash, Tweek, Wash, White Pony, Work, Working man's cocaine, Ya ba, Yellow bam, Yellow powder
AMPHETAMINES	Back dex, Bam, Bennie, Bens, Benz, Benzedrine, Benzidrine, Black and white, Black beauties, Black birds, Black bombers, Black cadillacs, Black mollies, Blacks, Blue boy, Blue mollies, Bolt, Brain pills, Brain ticklers, Brownies, Browns, Bumblebees, Cartwheels, Chicken powder, Christina, Co-pilot, Coasts to coasts, Crisscross, Cross tops, Crystal methadrine, Dex, Dexedrine, Dexies, Diamonds, Diet pills, Dolls, Dominoes, Double cross, Drivers, Eye openers, Fastin, Fives, Footballs, Forwards, French blue, Gaggler, Go, Greenies, Head drugs, Hearts, Horse heads, Hydro, Iboga, Inbetweens, Jam cecil, Jelly baby, Jelly bean, Jolly bean, Jugs, L.A., Leapers, Lid poppers, Lid proppers, Lightning, MAO, Marathons, Methedrine, Mini beans, Minibennie, Nugget, Oranges, Peaches, Pep pills, Pink hearts, Pixies, Pollutants, Rhythm, Rippers, Road dope, Rosa (Spanish), Roses, Snap, Snow pallets, Sparkle plenty, Sparklers, Speed, Spivias, Splash, Splivins, Strawberry shortcake, Sweeties, Tens, Thrusters, TR-6s, Truck drivers, Turnabout, U.S.P., Uppers, Uppies, Wake ups, West coast turnarounds, Whiffledust, White Cross

*Source: Office of National Drug Control Policy

▶ Stiff Penalties

Anyone who buys speed or meth better be prepared for serious consequences. Students caught with amphetamine or methamphetamine often are suspended or expelled from school. Others are kicked off their sports teams. Companies that require drug tests fire or refuse to hire speed and meth users.

According to federal law, it is illegal to sell or possess amphetamines and methamphetamine. Penalties are severe. A person caught with either drug, even on a first offense, could face up to a year in prison. Federal law mandates a five-year prison sentence for anyone who sells five to forty-nine grams of methamphetamine. For fifty or more grams, the sentence jumps to ten years.

Facing a meth crisis, Congress passed the Comprehensive Methamphetamine Control Act of 1996. This law permitted

▲ *Methamphetamine has become popular among young adults who attend raves.*

▲ *Crystal meth, or ice, is a pure, smokable form of methamphetamine. It looks like ice chips and is smoked using a glass pipe like the one shown in this picture.*

officials to seize chemicals used to make methamphetamine. It also increased penalties for trafficking such chemicals and for possessing meth-lab equipment.

In some states, lawmakers and prosecutors are turning up the heat on meth abusers. In Forsyth County, North Carolina, "we will put B1 felonies on anyone having anything to do with methamphetamines," said District Attorney Tom Keith.[7] A B1 felony means twelve years to life imprisonment. In Riverside County, California, a meth-abusing mother recently was charged with murder after her baby died from toxic breast milk.

In Tillman County, Oklahoma, highway patrol trooper Nik Green was killed in 2003. His alleged killer was a meth dealer. The murder inspired county authorities to crack down on meth users and producers. "Nik Green was Mr. Nice Guy, and Nik Green got killed," said Tillman County Sheriff Billy Hanes. "So we're not going to be Mr. Nice Guy anymore."[8]

FIGHTING SPEED AND METH ABUSE

According to one survey, 48.7 percent of American high school seniors did not think it would be a great risk to try crystal meth once or twice. They are deathly wrong. "The addiction is so strong . . . it pulls you to your grave," said Jenny Montague, a drug counselor in Arizona.[1] Amphetamine is a highly addictive drug, and meth is even more so. About 94 percent of those who smoke methamphetamine over a six-month period become addicted to it.[2]

For users, breaking free of their addiction is like a daily climb up Mount Everest. Still, with proper treatment and great willpower, addicts can conquer their addiction. "I have hope," said a meth addict named Iris. "I am sick and tired of being sick and tired, and I just want to feel alive again."[3]

▶ Warning Signs

After getting high on amphetamine just once, a person can become addicted to the drug. The same goes for methamphetamine. Many users enjoy their first high and think one more time cannot hurt. They then get high again, which entrenches them further into addiction. All across the land, doctors and counselors plead with young people: Do not start on these drugs!

Through seeing others' experiences, Tina's boyfriend knew how dangerous meth was. Yet, "he thought he could do it just once," she said. He did meth and lapsed into a coma. When he awoke, Tina said, "he was so severely brain damaged that he has no ability to do anything."[4] Anyone who has tried speed or meth one or more times and still desires the drug is battling addiction. They need to seek help immediately.

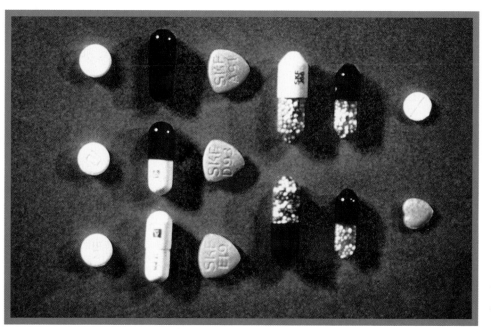

▲ *While amphetamines and methamphetamine may make a user feel happy and powerful at first, their withdrawal symptoms include severe depression and fatigue.*

Often, it is difficult to tell if friends or loved ones have a drug problem. They usually do all they can to hide their secret. Despite their deception, speed and meth abusers give off certain warning signs that they have a problem. They may lose weight or lose interest in eating. Their sleeping patterns may become abnormal. They might look disheveled, dirty, or sickly. They might skip school (or work) and become antisocial. Their grades could fall.

Speed and meth users might become fidgety, rude, testy, or volatile. They may appear depressed, panicked, or paranoid. They might ask to borrow money, beg for it, or even steal. Meth users may reek of chemicals. All of these signs indicate that they might have a problem with speed, meth, and/or another drug. They need to get help immediately.

▶ Where to Go for Help

If you believe your friend or loved one has a problem with speed or meth, you should not directly confront him or her. Meth abusers in particular can be extremely hostile, especially if they are in the tweaking stage. They have been known to attack and even kill those who confront them, including their spouses, their children, and armed police officers.

If you or someone you care about has a drug problem, you first should discuss it with an adult you can trust. This may be a parent or a relative. It also could be a teacher, a coach, or your doctor. Consider talking to your school counselor, who likely is trained to handle such matters. Often drug abusers are too scared or ashamed to discuss their problem with people they know. Help is available for them as well.

Those seeking help with addiction can contact NAADAC, the association of addiction professionals. It boasts the nation's largest network of alcohol- and drug-abuse treatment professionals. Other places to call include the Drug & Alcohol Treatment Referral National Hotline and the National Helplines. Narcotics Anonymous is a group that has aided many people into overcoming addictions. Another helpful organization is the Partnership for a Drug-Free America. You can contact these organizations by calling the phone numbers in the back of the book or by accessing the Web sites described in the front.

You also could check your local phone book. It might list a local drug treatment center, walk-in medical clinic, or crisis center. Some states offer methamphetamine hotlines. Moreover, you could contact your local library or hospital for advice. All of these sources boast experienced professionals who can help you.

▶ Treatment and Recovery

Typically, meth abusers are too heavily addicted to realize that they need to seek treatment on their own. Many do not enter treatment

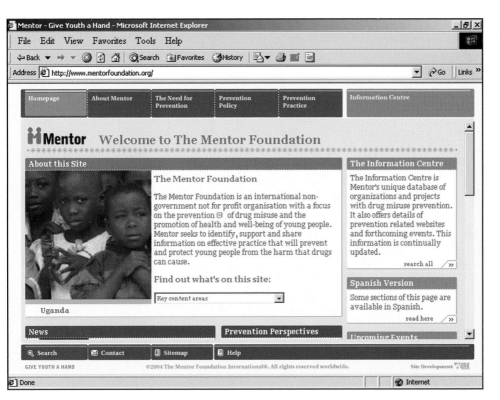

▲ Organizations such as the Mentor Foundation promote drug prevention and healthy lifestyles for young people.

until they are arrested and ordered to by a judge. Of course, it is best to enter treatment as early into the addiction as possible.

Treatment begins with a medical examination and psychological evaluation. Health care professionals likely will take tests and ask questions to determine the appropriate care. Normally, the doctor will have the patient go through a detoxification process in a hospital or treatment center. This is a difficult phase, but it is the only way to get the amphetamine or meth out of the patient's system. During withdrawal, which lasts days or even weeks, the patient will crave the drug intensely. She could become irritable, lethargic, depressed, and fearful. She might become nauseous, shake, sweat, and hyperventilate.

Once "detox" is over, many patients go through "rehab" at a drug treatment center. The goal at such a center is to repair patients physically, emotionally, and mentally. Patients are put on a healthy diet and begin to exercise. Through individual counseling and group therapy, they learn how to battle their addiction. Family counseling often is extremely important. Recovering addicts and their families need to mend the bonds that the drugs have destroyed.

A patient may spend several weeks in rehab. Afterward, he may live for months in a therapeutic community where his treatment continues. In relapse-prevention therapy, recovering addicts learn how to resist drugs and maintain a healthy lifestyle. They also learn how to avoid situations in which they are likely to use drugs. For many recovering addicts, resisting temptation is a lifelong battle.

▷ Making the Right Choices

You have now read about the horrors of amphetamine and methamphetamine. But what will you do if your friends ask you to try them? Peer pressure can be intense. In fact, you may find it easier to take the drug than to say "no" to your friends. Yet you must always remember this: That one small drug, taken for the first time, can destroy your life.

Here are some effective ways to refuse drugs:
- Give solid reasons: "No way. I just read about a kid who died from doing speed."
- Offer reasonable excuses: "I can't. I get drug-tested for football (or at work)."
- Suggest alternatives: "No, let's just watch TV."
- Do not get sucked into a discussion or argument. Just give them an emphatic "no."
- If talking does not work, just say goodbye and leave. Odds are, in a few days your friends will not remember or care about what happened. If they continue to press you, if

Activities such as hiking are healthier alternatives to taking amphetamines and methamphetamine. For some people, hiking provides all the pleasures of these drugs without their scary and dangerous side effects.

drugs are integral to the friendship, then it probably is time to let the friendship fizzle.

Nothing is cool about drugs. In fact, more than 90 percent of teenagers do not take drugs. Many who do wind up in an emergency room or jail sick, shaken, and scared.

Life offers plenty of natural highs. Young people can ski, swim, bike, or hike. They can sing and dance and laugh with friends. Those who are lonely or bored may find friends by joining a social club or after-school activity. Others may enjoy expressing themselves through music, writing, or acting. For many teens, doing volunteer work and helping others is the greatest feeling of all. These are choices that make young people feel good, not horribly ill.

Holly, the teenager mentioned at the beginning of this book, deeply regrets getting started on meth. Now she preaches against the drug. "I was lucky I made it out," she said. "Anybody who's doing it or dipping their toes into that puddle, it's not worth it. Stop it before it has a chance to start."[5]

addiction—Involuntary psychological, physical, or emotional dependence upon a substance that is known by the user to be harmful.

backyard burial—Secretly burying a body without notifying the proper authorities.

binge—An excessive indulgence of a substance without regard for the ill effects that the substance may cause.

clandestine—Something that is hidden or done in secret.

dopamine—A neurotransmitter, or chemical, in the brain that carries messages between brains cells and regulates physical movement, motivation, emotion, and pleasurable feelings.

drug paraphernalia—Accessory items that people use to carry, conceal, inject, smoke, or sniff drugs.

euphoria—Feeling of joy and good health.

fatigue—Temporary loss of strength and energy due to hard mental or physical labor, or stress.

hallucination—Visual perception of the presence of objects that are not real.

human immunodeficiency virus (HIV)—The virus that infects and destroys T cells in the immune system causing acquired immune deficiency syndrome (AIDS).

rape—Unlawful sexual activity conducted against the will of a person by force or threat of injury.

snort—Method of taking a drug by inhaling it in powdered form through the nostrils.

stimulant—A drug that causes increased activity of a person's organs.

Chapter 1. Speed, Meth, and Death

1. Janice Podsada, "The search for Holly begins," *The Herald,* February 11, 2002, <http://www.heraldnet.com/specialreports/methseries/files/stories/15057305.cfm> (December 27, 2003).

2. Ibid.

3. Janice Podsada, "Dying for a drug fix," *The Herald,* February 11, 2002, <http://www.heraldnet.com/specialreports/methseries/files/stories/15056308.cfm> (December 27, 2003).

4. Susie Ives, "Methamphetamine arrests are on the rise," *The Chronicle,* n.d., <http://www.omakchronicle.com/news/meth/meth1.html> (December 30, 2003).

5. "My Time's Up, It Didn't Have To Be This Way," *The Vaults of Erowid,* January 2, 2004, <http://www.erowid.org/experiences/exp.php?ID=25981> (December 28, 2003).

6. Ibid.

7. Joe Crea, "Crystal addict must hit bottom first," *The Washington Blade,* October 3, 2003, <http://www.aegis.com/news/wb/2003/WB031003.html> (December 28, 2003).

8. Iliana Limon, "Meth's Grip Fighting For Family," *The Albuquerque Tribune,* n.d., <http://www.abqtrib.com/archives/news04/011504_news_meth.shtml> (December 30, 2003).

9. Ibid.

10. "Effects of Meth Use Can Be Devastating," *KCI,* January 5, 2000, <http://www.kci.org/meth_info/sites/effects_of_meth.htm> (December 31, 2003).

Chapter 2. History of Speed and Meth

1. Liner notes, *The Essential Johnny Cash,* New York: Sony Music Entertainment, Inc., 2002.

2. "Interview With Johnny Cash," *CNN.com,* November 26, 2002, <http://www.cnn.com/TRANSCRIPTS/0211/26/lkl.00.html> (January 2, 2004).

3. Ibid.

4. National Institute on Drug Abuse, *Monitoring the Future: National Results on Adolescent Drug Use* (U.S. Department of Health and Human Services, 2003), p. 43.

5. Jon Bonné, "Scourge of the Heartland," *MSNBC,* n.d., <http://msnbc.msn.com/id/3071773> (January 4, 2004).

6. United States Department of Health and Human Services, "Other Illicit Drug Use," *Preliminary Results From the 1997 National Household Survey on Drug Abuse,* 1997, <http://www.oas.samhsa.gov/nhsda/nhsda97/nhsda981.htm> (July 14, 2004).

7. Sharon Cohen, "Easy to Make—If You're Careful," *The Daily Ardmoreite,* March 9, 1997, <http://ardmoreite.com/stories/030997/news/news13.html> (July 14, 2004).

8. Jon Bonné, "Meth's Deadly Buzz," *MSNBC,* n.d., <http://msnbc.msn.com/id/3071772> (January 4, 2004).

Chapter 3. Horrific Effects

1. Michelle Bradford and Pamela Hill, "The 'meth monster,'" *Arkansas Democrat-Gazette,* June 6, 1999, <http://www.ardemgaz.com/prev/meth0699/1amonster.asp> (January 5, 2004).

2. "Meth Hurts Families, Neighborhoods, Loved Ones," *Regional Drug Initiative,* n.d., <http://www.regionaldruginitiative.org/methbro.htm> (January 7, 2004).

3. "Effects of Meth Use Can Be Devastating," *KCI,* January 5, 2000, <http://www.kci.org/meth_info/sites/effects_of_meth.htm> (December 31, 2003).

4. Noaki Schwartz, "Surge in Meth Use Takes Toll on Rural Children," *Los Angeles Times,* May 7, 2001, <http://www.mapinc.org/drugnews/v01/n820/a06.html> (January 7, 2004).

5. Walter Kirn, "Crank," *Time,* June 22, 1998, p. 32.

6. Noaki Schwartz, "Surge in Meth Use Takes Toll on Rural Children," *Los Angeles Times,* May 7, 2001, <http://www.mapinc.org/drugnews/v01/n820/a06.html> (January 7, 2004).

7. Kimberly Mills, "The dangers of meth cannot be understated," *Seattle Post-Intelligencer,* December 13, 1999, <http://seattlepi.nwsource.com/methamphetamines/body.shtml> (January 5, 2004).

8. Noaki Schwartz, "Surge in Meth Use Takes Toll on Rural Children," *Los Angeles Times,* May 7, 2001, <http://www.mapinc.org/drugnews/v01/n820/a06.html> (January 7, 2004).

9. Ben A. Finley, "Meth a Master at Destroying Lives," *The Atlanta Journal-Constitution,* December 14, 2003, <http://www.ajc.com/metro/content/metro/meth/1203/14methletters.html> (January 9, 2004).

Chapter 4. Producing and Selling Speed and Meth

1. Anastasia Toufexis, "There Is No Safe Speed," *Time,* January 8, 1996, p. 37.

2. Jaymes Song, "Hawaii Has Huge Meth Mess," *The Associated Press,* September 12, 2003, <http://www.cbsnews.com/stories/2003/09/12/national/main573057.shtml> (January 12, 2004).

3. Chan Bailey as quoted on the NW HIDTA Web site, "Addiction: Crank: Made in America," *Mfiles: Meth and Marijuana Resource Tool,* n.d., <www.mfiles.org/Meth/user_impact/b2_addiction.html> (July 14, 2004).

4. Mike Patty, "Meth labs' youngest victims," *Rocky Mountain News,* January 20, 2004, <http://insidedenver.com/drmn/local/article/0,1299,DRMN_15_2589096,00.html> (January 11, 2004).

5. Ibid.

6. Steve Macko, "Methamphetamine Invades Middle America," *EmergencyNet,* April 13, 1997, <http://www.emergency.com/methinvd.htm> (January 11, 2004).

7. David Ingram, "Forsyth DA Will Also Try New Law," *Winston-Salem Journal,* July 20, 2003, <http://www.mapinc.org/drugnews/v03/n1106/a05.html> (January 12, 2004).

8. Trish Choate, "Gloves coming off in Tillman," *Times Record News,* January 23, 2004, <http://www.timesrecordnews.com/trn/local_news/article/0,1891,TRN_5784_259863,00.html> (January 16, 2004).

Chapter 5. Fighting Speed and Meth Abuse

1. Nate Searing, "A 'devil in disguise,'" *Sierra Vista Herald,* n.d., <http://www.svherald.com/articles/2003/08/30/news/news1.txt> (January 20, 2004).

2. "Amphetamines," Cape Town Drug Counselling Centre, n.d., <http://www.drugcentre.org.za/amphetamines.htm> (January 23, 2004).

3. Nate Searing, "Meth users have hard road to breaking drug habit," *Sierra Vista Herald,* n.d., <http://www.svherald.com/articles/2003/09/04/news/news2.txt> (January 20, 2004).

4. "Methamphetamine: Stories and Letters of the Hidden Costs," *KCI,* n.d., <http://www.kci.org/meth_info/letters/2003/September_2003.htm> (January 24, 2004).

5. Janice Podsada, "After Kicking Drugs, Girl's Life Forever Changed," *The Herald,* February 14, 2002, <http://www.heraldnet.com/specialreports/methseries/files/stories/15057308.cfm> (December 27, 2003).

Babbit, Nikki. *Adolescent Drug and Alcohol Abuse: How to Spot It, Stop It, and Get Help for Your Family.* Sebastopol, Calif.: O'Reilly & Associates, Inc., 2000.

Bayer, Linda N. *Amphetamines and Other Uppers.* Philadelphia: Chelsea House Publishers, 2000.

Clayton, Lawrence. *Amphetamines and Other Stimulants.* New York: Rosen Publishing Group, 2001.

Cobb, Allan B. *Speed and Your Brain: The Incredibly Disgusting Story.* New York: Rosen Central, 2000.

Connolly, Sean. *Amphetamines.* Chicago: Heinemann Library, 2000.

Elliot-Wright, Susan. *Amphetamines.* Chicago: Raintree, 2004.

Hyde, Margaret O. and John F. Setaro. *Drugs 101: An Overview.* Brookfield, Conn.: Twenty-First Century Books, 2003.

Kuhn, Cynthia, Scott Swartzwelder, and Wilkie Wilson. *Just Say Know: Talking With Kids about Drugs and Alcohol.* New York: Norton, W. W. & Company, Inc., 2002.

Lennard-Brown, Sarah. *Drugs.* Austin, Tex.: Raintree Steck-Vaughn Publishers, 2002.

Littell, Mary Anne. *Speed and Methamphetamine Drug Dangers.* Berkeley Heights, N.J.: Enslow Publishers, Inc., 2000.

Parker, Phillip M., ed., James N. Parker, ed. *The Official Patient's SourceBook on Methamphetamine Dependence.* San Diego: ICON Health Publications, 2002.

Pellowski, Michael J. *Amphetamine Drug Dangers.* Berkeley Heights, N.J.: Enslow Publishers, Inc., 2001.

Phone Numbers

NAADAC, the Association of Addiction Professionals
(800) 548–0497

Drug & Alcohol Treatment Referral National Hotline
(800) 662–4357

National Helplines
(800) HELP–111

Narcotics Anonymous
(818) 773–9999

Partnership for a Drug-Free America
(212) 922–1560